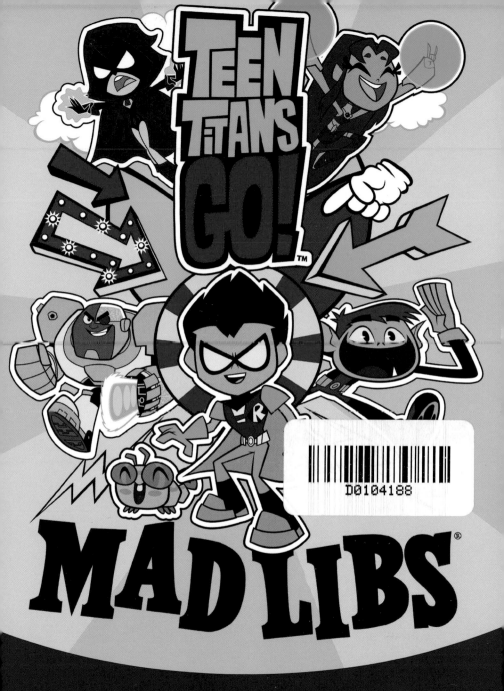

TEEN TITANS GO!™

MAD LIBS®

World's Greatest Word Game

MAD LIBS

by Eric Luper

Mad Libs
An Imprint of Penguin Random House

MAD LIBS
Penguin Young Readers Group
An Imprint of Penguin Random House LLC

Mad Libs format copyright © 2017 by Penguin Random House LLC. All rights reserved.

Concept created by Roger Price & Leonard Stern

Copyright © 2017 DC Comics.TEEN TITANS GO! and all related characters and elements
© & ™ DC Comics and Warner Bros. Entertainment Inc. (s17)

Published by Mad Libs,
an imprint of Penguin Random House LLC,
345 Hudson Street, New York, New York 10014.
Printed in the USA.

ISBN 9780399542220
5 7 9 10 8 6 4

MAD LIBS

INSTRUCTIONS

MAD LIBS® is a game for people who don't like games!
It can be played by one, two, three, four, or forty.

● RIDICULOUSLY SIMPLE DIRECTIONS

In this tablet you will find stories containing blank spaces where words
are left out. One player, the READER, selects one of these stories. The
READER does not tell anyone what the story is about. Instead, he/she asks
the other players, the WRITERS, to give him/her words. These words are
used to fill in the blank spaces in the story.

● TO PLAY

The READER asks each WRITER in turn to call out a word—an adjective or
a noun or whatever the space calls for—and uses them to fill in the blank
spaces in the story. The result is a MAD LIBS® game.

When the READER then reads the completed MAD LIBS® game to the other
players, they will discover that they have written a story that is fantastic,
screamingly funny, shocking, silly, crazy, or just plain dumb—depending
upon which words each WRITER called out.

● EXAMPLE (*Before* and *After*)

"_____ !" he said _____
       EXCLAMATION   ADVERB

as he jumped into his convertible _____ and
                                          NOUN

drove off with his _____ wife.
                       ADJECTIVE

"_____ OUCH _____ !" he said _____ STUPIDLY _____
       EXCLAMATION   ADVERB

as he jumped into his convertible _____ CAT _____ and
                                          NOUN

drove off with his _____ BRAVE _____ wife.
                       ADJECTIVE

In case you have forgotten what adjectives, adverbs, nouns, and verbs are, here is a quick review:

An ADJECTIVE describes something or somebody. *Lumpy, soft, ugly, messy,* and *short* are adjectives.

An ADVERB tells how something is done. It modifies a verb and usually ends in "ly." *Modestly, stupidly, greedily,* and *carefully* are adverbs.

A NOUN is the name of a person, place, or thing. *Sidewalk, umbrella, bridle, bathtub,* and *nose* are nouns.

A VERB is an action word. *Run, pitch, jump,* and *swim* are verbs. Put the verbs in past tense if the directions say PAST TENSE. *Ran, pitched, jumped,* and *swam* are verbs in the past tense.

When we ask for A PLACE, we mean any sort of place: a country or city (*Spain, Cleveland*) or a room (*bathroom, kitchen*).

An EXCLAMATION or SILLY WORD is any sort of funny sound, gasp, grunt, or outcry, like *Wow!, Ouch!, Whomp!, Ick!,* and *Gadzooks!*

When we ask for specific words, like a NUMBER, a COLOR, an ANIMAL, or a PART OF THE BODY, we mean a word that is one of those things, like *seven, blue, horse,* or *head.*

When we ask for a PLURAL, it means more than one. For example, *cat* pluralized is *cats.*

MAD LIBS® is fun to play with friends, but you can also play it by yourself! To begin with, DO NOT look at the story on the page below. Fill in the blanks on this page with the words called for. Then, using the words you have selected, fill in the blank spaces in the story.

Now you've created your own hilarious MAD LIBS® game!

THE TEEN TITANS AT HOME

PLURAL NOUN _____

A PLACE _____

ADJECTIVE _____

PERSON IN ROOM _____

VERB _____

PART OF THE BODY (PLURAL) _____

VERB ENDING IN "ING" _____

NOUN _____

NOUN _____

VERB _____

ADJECTIVE _____

VERB _____

VERB _____

NUMBER _____

PLURAL NOUN _____

VERB _____

VERB _____

ADJECTIVE _____

THE TEEN TITANS AT HOME

When they are not busy defeating _____, the Teen Titans
PLURAL NOUN

love hanging out in their _____. I mean, it's totally
A PLACE

_____ to take down Gizmo, Billy Numerous, or
ADJECTIVE

_____, but super heroes need to _____ and
PERSON IN ROOM   VERB

put up their _____, too! Even when they're
PART OF THE BODY (PLURAL)

_____ at home, Robin still likes to think he's the
VERB ENDING IN "ING"

_____, while Cyborg and Beast Boy just sit on the
NOUN

_____ and _____ video games. Raven watches *Pretty*
NOUN   VERB

_____ *Pegasus*, and Starfire makes chili for everyone to
ADJECTIVE

_____. Of course, they get called to _____
VERB   VERB

emergencies sometimes, but did you think it was all fighting the

H.I.V.E. _____ and saving the world from _____?
NUMBER   PLURAL NOUN

The Titans work hard, but they also _____ hard. So, when
VERB

there's trouble, you know who to _____! The _____
VERB   ADJECTIVE

Titans!

MAD LIBS® is fun to play with friends, but you can also play it by yourself! To begin with, DO NOT look at the story on the page below. Fill in the blanks on this page with the words called for. Then, using the words you have selected, fill in the blank spaces in the story.

Now you've created your own hilarious MAD LIBS® game!

SO, YOU WANT TO BE A TEEN TITAN?

NOUN _____

PART OF THE BODY (PLURAL) _____

VERB ENDING IN "ING" _____

ADJECTIVE _____

ADVERB _____

VERB _____

NOUN _____

CELEBRITY _____

NOUN _____

ADJECTIVE _____

ADJECTIVE _____

COLOR _____

SILLY WORD _____

MAD○LIBS
SO, YOU WANT TO BE A TEEN TITAN?

Do you have what it takes to be a Teen Titan? It's no easy _____

NOUN

to be one. Sure, it may look like they sit around all day on their

_____ watching TV and _____

PART OF THE BODY (PLURAL)   VERB ENDING IN "ING"

around, but being a super hero is no _____ business.

ADJECTIVE

- You need to be _____ brave. If there's a problem, will

ADVERB

  you _____ under your bed, or will you jump up to face

VERB

  the _____?

NOUN

- You need strength. You can't take on Mammoth or _____

CELEBRITY

  without a little power in your _____!

NOUN

- You need a/an _____ costume. No super hero is

ADJECTIVE

  _____ without one. Will it be blue or black? Maybe

ADJECTIVE

  pink with a/an _____ cape? The choice is up to you!

COLOR

- You need a catchphrase. "Boo-Yah!" and "Bam!" are already

  taken. Why don't you try _____?

SILLY WORD

MAD LIBS® is fun to play with friends, but you can also play it by yourself! To begin with, DO NOT look at the story on the page below. Fill in the blanks on this page with the words called for. Then, using the words you have selected, fill in the blank spaces in the story.

Now you've created your own hilarious MAD LIBS® game!

CONFESSIONS OF THE BOY WONDER!

ADJECTIVE _____

VERB ENDING IN "ING" _____

COLOR _____

TYPE OF FOOD _____

VERB _____

ADJECTIVE _____

ARTICLE OF CLOTHING _____

ADJECTIVE _____

NOUN _____

VERB ENDING IN "ING" _____

PLURAL NOUN _____

VERB _____

A PLACE _____

NOUN _____

PLURAL NOUN _____

VERB _____

NOUN _____

MAD LIBS
CONFESSIONS OF THE
BOY WONDER!

There's only so long a/an _____ guy can be a sidekick. Sure,
                              ADJECTIVE

there are plenty of benefits to _____ out with a
                                 VERB ENDING IN "ING"

billionaire who wears a/an _____ mask. Free car, free mansion,
                             COLOR

and all the _____ you can eat! But I just got so sick of
              TYPE OF FOOD

hearing "Robin, do this. Robin, _____ that." So, I grabbed
                                  VERB

my _____ tights and a/an _____, and I
     ADJECTIVE   ARTICLE OF CLOTHING

formed the _____ super hero group the Teen Titans. It's not easy
             ADJECTIVE

being the _____ of this group. We should be
            NOUN

_____ evil 24/7, but my _____ just want
VERB ENDING IN "ING"   PLURAL NOUN

to _____ around. Plus, try living in a/an _____ with
     VERB   A PLACE

Starfire, who happens to be the _____ of my dreams! But it's all
                                  NOUN

good. Now I get to call the _____. I get to _____
                              PLURAL NOUN   VERB

what the team does. I get to call myself _____ of the Teen Titans!
                                           NOUN

MAD LIBS® is fun to play with friends, but you can also play it by yourself! To begin with, DO NOT look at the story on the page below. Fill in the blanks on this page with the words called for. Then, using the words you have selected, fill in the blank spaces in the story.

Now you've created your own hilarious MAD LIBS® game!

BEWARE THE H.I.V.E. FIVE!

ADJECTIVE _____

NOUN _____

ADJECTIVE _____

ADJECTIVE _____

VERB _____

ADJECTIVE _____

PLURAL NOUN _____

PART OF THE BODY _____

ADJECTIVE _____

VEHICLE _____

VERB _____

PLURAL NOUN _____

PART OF THE BODY _____

NUMBER _____

VERB _____

A PLACE _____

MAD LIBS

BEWARE THE H.I.V.E. FIVE!

The H.I.V.E. Five is a group of villains with one _____ goal:
ADJECTIVE

to defeat the Teen Titans!

- **Gizmo:** He's the leader of the _____. He's really
NOUN

_____ with technology, but he's sensitive about his size.
ADJECTIVE

He may be _____, but don't _____ with him!
ADJECTIVE   VERB

- **Jinx:** The only girl in the H.I.V.E. Five, Jinx uses her

_____ Optic Blasts to give her _____ bad
ADJECTIVE   PLURAL NOUN

luck! Gotta love her pink _____!
PART OF THE BODY

- **Mammoth:** Mammoth is known for his _____
ADJECTIVE

strength! He's like a/an _____ with arms and legs
VEHICLE

who is always ready to _____ his enemies!
VERB

- **See-More:** With his eye helmet, See-More shoots _____
PLURAL NOUN

from his large _____. Watch out!
PART OF THE BODY

- **Billy Numerous:** Is he two, four, six, or _____? Billy
NUMBER

can _____ himself into more people than you could fit
VERB

into (the) _____!
A PLACE

MAD LIBS® is fun to play with friends, but you can also play it by yourself! To begin with, DO NOT look at the story on the page below. Fill in the blanks on this page with the words called for. Then, using the words you have selected, fill in the blank spaces in the story.

Now you've created your own hilarious MAD LIBS® game!

RECIPE TO MAKE A LEGENDARY SANDWICH!

ADJECTIVE _____

VERB _____

TYPE OF FOOD _____

A PLACE _____

ADJECTIVE _____

ADJECTIVE _____

NOUN _____

ADJECTIVE _____

A PLACE _____

ADJECTIVE _____

SILLY WORD _____

NOUN _____

TYPE OF FOOD _____

ADJECTIVE _____

NOUN _____

MAD LIBS
RECIPE TO MAKE A
LEGENDARY SANDWICH!

The Book of _____ Legends speaks of a sandwich that would
                ADJECTIVE

allow an old king to _____ his kingdom forever. However,
                     VERB

when the king caught the prince trying to steal the _____,
                                                    TYPE OF FOOD

he had it pulled apart. The ingredients were hidden in the far corners

of (the) _____. _____ guardians may protect these
         A PLACE   ADJECTIVE

ingredients, but we have uncovered the _____ recipe for the
                                       ADJECTIVE

_____ of Power:
NOUN

- **Mystical Bacon:** Some might say that *all* bacon is mystical, but

  this bacon hidden at Lava Lake is the most _____ of all!
                                             ADJECTIVE

- **King's Lettuce:** This lettuce, buried in an underground

  _____, is crispy and _____.
  A PLACE   ADJECTIVE

- **Stellar Tomato:** Hidden on a planet in the _____
                                                SILLY WORD

  System, this _____ is sliced thin and juicy.
               NOUN

- **Pretzel Bread:** Okay, pretzel _____ is not magical, but
                                   TYPE OF FOOD

  it's yummy. You can find it at the _____ supermarket.
                                     ADJECTIVE

Put these ingredients together and you've got the best _____
                                                       NOUN

in the universe!

From TEEN TITANS GO! MAD LIBS® • © & ™ DC Comics and Warner Bros. Entertainment Inc. (s17).
Published in 2017 by Mad Libs, an imprint of Penguin Random House LLC.

MAD LIBS® is fun to play with friends, but you can also play it by yourself! To begin with, DO NOT look at the story on the page below. Fill in the blanks on this page with the words called for. Then, using the words you have selected, fill in the blank spaces in the story.

Now you've created your own hilarious MAD LIBS® game!

STARFIRE: HALF TEEN, ALL ALIEN!

ADJECTIVE _____

NOUN _____

PLURAL NOUN _____

VERB _____

PART OF THE BODY (PLURAL) _____

PLURAL NOUN _____

A PLACE _____

ADVERB _____

ADJECTIVE _____

VERB _____

NOUN _____

ADJECTIVE _____

CELEBRITY _____

NOUN _____

Starfire is a/an _____ member of the Teen Titans. She
ADJECTIVE

is a princess from the planet Tamaran, but now calls Earth her

_____. She has superhuman _____ and can
NOUN _PLURAL NOUN_

_____ around in the sky. She can also shoot starbolts out of
VERB

her _____ and _____ from her eyes.
PART OF THE BODY (PLURAL) _PLURAL NOUN_

Starfire can even survive in (the) _____! Despite being
A PLACE

_____ powerful, Starfire is also kindhearted and
ADVERB

_____. If she wasn't, she might _____ the whole
ADJECTIVE _VERB_

world before anyone could stop her! Starfire always tells the

_____ and has trouble saying anything _____ about
NOUN _ADJECTIVE_

anyone, even _____! It's not easy to get Starfire angry, but
CELEBRITY

when she is . . . watch out! She is a/an _____ to be reckoned
NOUN

with.

MAD LIBS® is fun to play with friends, but you can also play it by yourself! To begin with, DO NOT look at the story on the page below. Fill in the blanks on this page with the words called for. Then, using the words you have selected, fill in the blank spaces in the story.

Now you've created your own hilarious MAD LIBS® game!

POWER MOVES!

ADJECTIVE _____

NUMBER _____

VERB _____

ADJECTIVE _____

NOUN _____

ADVERB _____

A PLACE _____

ANIMAL _____

PERSON IN ROOM _____

PART OF THE BODY _____

TYPE OF FOOD _____

NOUN _____

CELEBRITY _____

PLURAL NOUN _____

COLOR _____

SILLY WORD _____

MAD LIBS

POWER MOVES!

Each Teen Titan has their own _____ powers, but what
                                   ADJECTIVE

happens when all _____ of them _____ their powers
                     NUMBER   VERB

together to make extreme superpowers?

- The **Power Rang** is when Cyborg's _____ Cannon
                                          ADJECTIVE

  and Robin's _____ combine to form a weapon strong
                   NOUN

  enough to _____ destroy (the) _____.
                  ADVERB   A PLACE

  Kaboom!

- The **Thunder Alley KO** is when Beast Boy turns into a/an

  _____ and rolls the head of _____ at a villain.
       ANIMAL   PERSON IN ROOM

  Kapow!

- The **Flying Soda Grab** is when Cyborg picks up Robin

  and extends his _____ so he can grab
                        PART OF THE BODY

  _____ from the fridge. Boo-Yah!
     TYPE OF FOOD

- The **Ultimate Power** _____ is when _____
                             NOUN   CELEBRITY

  turns into a triceratops, and Starfire rides on its back. Raven

  uses _____ to make _____ armor and a
          PLURAL NOUN   COLOR

  sword. _____!
            SILLY WORD

MAD LIBS® is fun to play with friends, but you can also play it by yourself! To begin with, DO NOT look at the story on the page below. Fill in the blanks on this page with the words called for. Then, using the words you have selected, fill in the blank spaces in the story.

Now you've created your own hilarious MAD LIBS® game!

A TOUR OF TITANS TOWER

NOUN _____

ADJECTIVE _____

A PLACE _____

VERB _____

ADJECTIVE _____

VERB ENDING IN "ING" _____

NOUN _____

CELEBRITY _____

PLURAL NOUN _____

VERB _____

VERB _____

NOUN _____

TYPE OF FOOD _____

NUMBER _____

MAD LIBS

A TOUR OF TITANS TOWER

Shaped like a giant _____, Titans Tower is the
NOUN

_____ home of the Teen Titans. Located near the water close
ADJECTIVE

to (the) _____, the Titans live here ready to _____ any
A PLACE   VERB

trouble that comes their way. Each Titan has their own _____
ADJECTIVE

bedroom, but they usually hang out in the _____
VERB ENDING IN "ING"

room. This is where the Titans watch television and sit on the

_____. Then there's the kitchen. This is the favorite room of
NOUN

Cyborg and _____. The Titans love to eat _____
CELEBRITY   PLURAL NOUN

in there—sometimes they even _____ there, too! So
VERB

_____ by anytime. The _____ is always open, there's
VERB   NOUN

always _____ to eat, and the thermostat is set at a comfy
TYPE OF FOOD

_____ degrees!
NUMBER

MAD LIBS® is fun to play with friends, but you can also play it by yourself! To begin with, DO NOT look at the story on the page below. Fill in the blanks on this page with the words called for. Then, using the words you have selected, fill in the blank spaces in the story.

Now you've created your own hilarious MAD LIBS® game!

STARING AT THE FUTURE

VERB ENDING IN "ING" _____

NOUN _____

TYPE OF FOOD _____

ADJECTIVE _____

VERB ENDING IN "ING" _____

NOUN _____

NUMBER _____

PLURAL NOUN _____

OCCUPATION _____

ADJECTIVE _____

A PLACE _____

NOUN _____

ADJECTIVE _____

VERB _____

PLURAL NOUN _____

VERB _____

ADJECTIVE _____

MAD LIBS

STARING AT THE FUTURE

Can _____ the last slice of pizza really change the
     VERB ENDING IN "ING"

future of the world? Cyborg and Beast _____ find out when
                                         NOUN

they go to the local _____ restaurant. Trouble follows
                        TYPE OF FOOD

when they argue over who gets the last _____ slice. They
                                          ADJECTIVE

decide to have a/an _____ contest: winner gets the
                     VERB ENDING IN "ING"

_____. _____ years go by. Robin is married with
    NOUN   NUMBER

_____. Starfire is the _____ of Tamaran.
  PLURAL NOUN   OCCUPATION

Raven is a cloud of _____ cosmic energy and keeps
                        ADJECTIVE

(the) _____ in balance. Cyborg and Beast Boy decide to build
      A PLACE

a/an _____ machine to go back in time and change the future
       NOUN

so that no one will have _____ responsibilities. Instead of staring
                          ADJECTIVE

at the pizza, they _____ it. Thirty years later, the world is
                      VERB

filled with _____. Chaos reigns. And Cyborg and Beast
             PLURAL NOUN

Boy can _____ happily, knowing they saved everyone from
           VERB

their _____ responsibilities!
        ADJECTIVE

MAD LIBS® is fun to play with friends, but you can also play it by yourself! To begin with, DO NOT look at the story on the page below. Fill in the blanks on this page with the words called for. Then, using the words you have selected, fill in the blank spaces in the story.

Now you've created your own hilarious MAD LIBS® game!

CYBORG: HALF TEEN, HALF ROBOT!

ADJECTIVE _____

NOUN _____

NOUN _____

NOUN _____

VERB _____

PART OF THE BODY _____

PART OF THE BODY _____

PART OF THE BODY _____

TYPE OF FOOD _____

ADJECTIVE _____

VERB _____

ADVERB _____

NOUN _____

ADJECTIVE _____

ADJECTIVE _____

MAD LIBS®
CYBORG: HALF TEEN, HALF ROBOT!

If anyone is the _____ powerhouse of the Teen Titans, it's
                        ADJECTIVE

Cyborg. Part human, mostly _____, this Titan has no trouble
                              NOUN

getting the _____ done! He is super-strong, immune to the
                NOUN

hottest _____, and he can _____ through the air. He
              NOUN   VERB

can fire missiles from his _____ and lasers from his
                              PART OF THE BODY

_____! He can take photos with his eye and print
   PART OF THE BODY

them out with his _____. Plus, he can make
                        PART OF THE BODY

_____ come out of his arm! Even though only his head is
   TYPE OF FOOD

human, Cyborg is always _____. He wants to eat and
                            ADJECTIVE

_____ and eat some more! But Cyborg is also _____
      VERB   ADVERB

smart. He can take apart a complicated _____ and put it back
                                          NOUN

together again. He's an expert with _____ technology, too!
                                        ADJECTIVE

So, don't just think of Cyborg as a/an _____ strongman. He's
                                          ADJECTIVE

far more than that!

MAD LIBS® is fun to play with friends, but you can also play it by yourself! To begin with, DO NOT look at the story on the page below. Fill in the blanks on this page with the words called for. Then, using the words you have selected, fill in the blank spaces in the story.

Now you've created your own hilarious MAD LIBS® game!

TITANS' FAVORITE ACTIVITIES

ADJECTIVE _____

A PLACE _____

ADVERB _____

VERB _____

NOUN _____

PART OF THE BODY _____

NOUN _____

TYPE OF FOOD _____

NUMBER _____

EXCLAMATION _____

VERB ENDING IN "ING" _____

VERB _____

ADJECTIVE _____

ADJECTIVE _____

VERB ENDING IN "ING" _____

MAD LIBS®
TITANS' FAVORITE ACTIVITIES

The Teen Titans have many interests when they are not protecting

Jump City from _____ evil. After all, it's not all putting bad
  _____ADJECTIVE_____

guys in (the) _____! For example, Beast Boy and Cyborg like
  ___A PLACE___

to eat _____. They also like to _____ on the couch
  __ADVERB__   __VERB__

so they can play their favorite _____ games. Raven loves to
  ____NOUN____

read. She always has her _____ buried in a book. She
  __PART OF THE BODY__

also loves watching her favorite _____, *Pretty Pretty Pegasus*.
  ____NOUN____

Starfire enjoys being polite and cooking _____ in the
  __TYPE OF FOOD__

toilet. And, of course, Robin enjoys exercising. He can do _____
  __NUMBER__

pull-ups in a minute! _____! Silkie just loves
  __EXCLAMATION__

_____ around. And did I mention Cyborg and Beast
__VERB ENDING IN "ING"__

Boy like to eat and _____ video games? No, the Teen Titans
  __VERB__

aren't your average _____ heroes. They have many other
  __ADJECTIVE__

_____ interests—like eating and _____ video
__ADJECTIVE__   __VERB ENDING IN "ING"__

games!

MAD LIBS® is fun to play with friends, but you can also play it by yourself! To begin with, DO NOT look at the story on the page below. Fill in the blanks on this page with the words called for. Then, using the words you have selected, fill in the blank spaces in the story.

Now you've created your own hilarious MAD LIBS® game!

ROBIN AND STARFIRE

FIRST NAME (FEMALE) _____

VERB _____

NOUN _____

ADJECTIVE _____

ADJECTIVE _____

NOUN _____

PLURAL NOUN _____

ADJECTIVE _____

FIRST NAME (MALE) _____

A PLACE _____

MAD LIBS®

ROBIN AND STARFIRE

People think Romeo and _____ are the most famous
FIRST NAME (FEMALE)

couple in history, but that's totally untrue! Now there's Robin and

Starfire! Okay, it's true . . . Robin does _____ Starfire more
VERB

than she likes him. In fact, she only likes him like a/an _____.
NOUN

Bummer! Good thing Robin's _____ love for Starfire is enough
ADJECTIVE

for the two of them. It's okay that Robin doesn't have a/an _____
ADJECTIVE

sense of humor; Starfire rarely understands the _____ anyway.
NOUN

Maybe her humor is better suited to the _____ of Tamaran.
PLURAL NOUN

Plus, they are two of the most _____ Titans in the group. Talk
ADJECTIVE

about a power couple! So step aside, _____ and Juliet.
FIRST NAME (MALE)

Robin and Starfire are a match made in (the) _____!
A PLACE

From TEEN TITANS GO! MAD LIBS® • © & ™ DC Comics and Warner Bros. Entertainment Inc. (s17).
Published in 2017 by Mad Libs, an imprint of Penguin Random House LLC.

MAD LIBS® is fun to play with friends, but you can also play it by yourself! To begin with, DO NOT look at the story on the page below. Fill in the blanks on this page with the words called for. Then, using the words you have selected, fill in the blank spaces in the story.

Now you've created your own hilarious MAD LIBS® game!

RAVEN, HALF TEEN, HALF DEMON

ADJECTIVE _____

NOUN _____

PLURAL NOUN _____

PLURAL NOUN _____

PART OF THE BODY _____

NOUN _____

NOUN _____

ADJECTIVE _____

ADVERB _____

VERB _____

ADJECTIVE _____

ADVERB _____

VERB ENDING IN "ING" _____

PLURAL NOUN _____

ADJECTIVE _____

ADJECTIVE _____

VERB _____

SILLY WORD _____

MAD LIBS
RAVEN, HALF TEEN, HALF DEMON

Perhaps the darkest and most _____ member of the Teen
                            ADJECTIVE

Titans is Raven. She is half human, half _____, and has the
                                          NOUN

_____ of both. Raven can fly. She also has telekinesis,
PLURAL NOUN

which means she can move _____ with her
                              PLURAL NOUN

_____. When she does, the _____ is
PART OF THE BODY   NOUN

covered in a dark _____. She can also create _____
                     NOUN   ADJECTIVE

objects out of thin air with her powers. Raven can _____ cast
                                                      ADVERB

magical spells. All she needs to do is say, "Azarath Metrion Zinthos!"

and she is able to _____ clones or give life to _____
                      VERB   ADJECTIVE

objects. Raven's relationship with Beast Boy is _____ complex.
                                                   ADVERB

One day she ignores him because he's _____ like a
                                        VERB ENDING IN "ING"

baby. The next, she shows him _____. How confusing!
                                  PLURAL NOUN

At the end of the day, Raven is a/an _____ part of the team.
                                        ADJECTIVE

Without her, the _____ Titans might _____ apart.
                    ADJECTIVE   VERB

When Raven yells "_____," the bad guys better watch out!
                     SILLY WORD

From TEEN TITANS GO! MAD LIBS® • © & ™ DC Comics and Warner Bros. Entertainment Inc. (s17).
Published in 2017 by Mad Libs, an imprint of Penguin Random House LLC.

MAD LIBS® is fun to play with friends, but you can also play it by yourself! To begin with, DO NOT look at the story on the page below. Fill in the blanks on this page with the words called for. Then, using the words you have selected, fill in the blank spaces in the story.

Now you've created your own hilarious MAD LIBS® game!

LOVE MONSTERS

VERB _____

PLURAL NOUN _____

ADJECTIVE _____

VERB _____

COLOR _____

ADJECTIVE _____

PART OF THE BODY (PLURAL) _____

A PLACE _____

TYPE OF FOOD _____

NOUN _____

ADJECTIVE _____

NOUN _____

PLURAL NOUN _____

VERB _____

LOVE MONSTERS

Raven gives a small chest to the other Titans, but warns them not to

_____ it. Inside are the Twin Destroyers of Azarath, who feed
VERB

on love and _____! After Raven leaves, Starfire wants to
PLURAL NOUN

open the chest. After all, what could be _____ inside such a
ADJECTIVE

tiny chest? After she opens it, two fuzzy creatures _____ out.
VERB

They are green and _____, and they both have big
COLOR

_____ _____. So cute! The Titans have fun
ADJECTIVE   PART OF THE BODY (PLURAL)

with them, taking them to (the) _____ and giving them
A PLACE

_____ to eat. At the end of the day, Starfire insists on
TYPE OF FOOD

giving the creatures one last _____. That was not such a/an
NOUN

_____ idea, because they turn into a/an _____ that
ADJECTIVE   NOUN

hatches into a two-headed monster! After the Titans defeat the

monster, it turns back into two cute _____. So cute that
PLURAL NOUN

Starfire must _____ them again. Nooooo!
VERB

From TEEN TITANS GO! MAD LIBS® • © & ™ DC Comics and Warner Bros. Entertainment Inc. (s17).
Published in 2017 by Mad Libs, an imprint of Penguin Random House LLC.

MAD LIBS® is fun to play with friends, but you can also play it by yourself! To begin with, DO NOT look at the story on the page below. Fill in the blanks on this page with the words called for. Then, using the words you have selected, fill in the blank spaces in the story.

Now you've created your own hilarious MAD LIBS® game!

ROBIN'S STUFF, AN INVENTORY LIST

ADJECTIVE _____

VERB _____

ADJECTIVE _____

PLURAL NOUN _____

PART OF THE BODY _____

NOUN _____

SILLY WORD _____

ADJECTIVE _____

NOUN _____

VERB _____

PERSON IN ROOM _____

VERB _____

VEHICLE _____

Since Robin has no _____ powers, he relies on special gear.
ADJECTIVE

Let's look at what he uses to _____ villains:
VERB

- **Birdarangs:** Maybe Robin's most _____ weapon, he
  ADJECTIVE

  throws them at his foes to stop them in their _____!
  PLURAL NOUN

- **Staff:** This is a long pole used for hand-to-_____
  PART OF THE BODY

  combat and vaulting into the _____.
  NOUN

- **Smoke Bombs:** Throw a few of these and "_____!"
  SILLY WORD

  You've disappeared into _____ air! And gotten
  ADJECTIVE

  smoke on your newly washed _____.
  NOUN

- **Grappling Hook:** As the only Titan who can't fly, Robin

  needs these to _____ to high places. That is, when
  VERB

  _____ doesn't carry him.
  PERSON IN ROOM

- **Vehicles:** Robin has been known to _____ a motorcycle,
  VERB

  a car, a sub, and a/an _____.
  VEHICLE

MAD LIBS® is fun to play with friends, but you can also play it by yourself! To begin with, DO NOT look at the story on the page below. Fill in the blanks on this page with the words called for. Then, using the words you have selected, fill in the blank spaces in the story.

Now you've created your own hilarious MAD LIBS® game!

BEAST BOY: HALF TEEN, HALF ANYTHING ELSE!

ANIMAL _____

VERB ENDING IN "ING" _____

ADJECTIVE _____

ANIMAL _____

PART OF THE BODY (PLURAL) _____

ADJECTIVE _____

VERB _____

PERSON IN ROOM _____

ADJECTIVE _____

CELEBRITY (FEMALE) _____

VERB _____

VERB ENDING IN "ING" _____

PLURAL NOUN _____

A PLACE _____

ADJECTIVE _____

MAD LIBS
BEAST BOY: HALF TEEN, HALF ANYTHING ELSE!

If you see a big green _____ walking through your town,
                          ANIMAL

chances are you're _____ at Beast Boy! Beast Boy is the
                   VERB ENDING IN "ING"

smallest of the Titans, but he's certainly not the most _____.
                                                         ADJECTIVE

Whether it's a dinosaur or a/an _____, he can turn into any
                                ANIMAL

creature he wants. Even though he has green skin, hair, and

_____, Beast Boy is still a cute, _____ guy.
PART OF THE BODY (PLURAL)   ADJECTIVE

He's always laughing and loves to _____ pranks on his friends,
                                  VERB

like that time when he led _____ to believe he was
                           PERSON IN ROOM

_____! Beast Boy is in love with _____, and
ADJECTIVE   CELEBRITY (FEMALE)

he'd do anything for her to _____ him back. Beast Boy is also
                            VERB

good at writing poetry, _____ the guitar, and drawing
                        VERB ENDING IN "ING"

_____. Add to that his love for video games and hanging
PLURAL NOUN

out in (the) _____, and he might be the most _____
             A PLACE   ADJECTIVE

Titan of them all!

MAD LIBS® is fun to play with friends, but you can also play it by yourself! To begin with, DO NOT look at the story on the page below. Fill in the blanks on this page with the words called for. Then, using the words you have selected, fill in the blank spaces in the story.

Now you've created your own hilarious MAD LIBS® game!

TITANS EAST

NOUN _____

VERB _____

ANIMAL _____

VERB _____

ADJECTIVE _____

PLURAL NOUN _____

PERSON IN ROOM _____

VERB ENDING IN "ING" _____

NOUN _____

ADJECTIVE _____

PLURAL NOUN _____

ADJECTIVE _____

VERB _____

ADJECTIVE _____

NOUN _____

A PLACE _____

ADVERB _____

MAD LIBS

TITANS EAST

Whether you believe it or not, there's a whole other _____

NOUN

of teen heroes on the East Coast called Titans East.

- **Bumblebee** is the leader of the group. She can _____

VERB

  to the size of an actual _____. She can _____

ANIMAL VERB

  through the air and shoot _____ stingers at her

ADJECTIVE

  _____!

PLURAL NOUN

- **Speedy** is very much like _____. He is skilled at

PERSON IN ROOM

  fighting and _____ and is a master of the bow

VERB ENDING IN "ING"

  and _____.

NOUN

- **Aqualad** is the most _____ when he's underwater. He

ADJECTIVE

  can swim quickly and control _____. Plus, he's

PLURAL NOUN

  a/an _____ DJ!

ADJECTIVE

- And who can _____ **Mas y Menos**, whose names mean

VERB

  "more" and "_____" in Spanish? **Mas y Menos** both

ADJECTIVE

  love tamales and speed around faster than a/an _____.

NOUN

So if there's trouble on the east side of (the) _____, count on

A PLACE

Titans East to _____ save the day!

ADVERB

From TEEN TITANS GO! MAD LIBS® • © & ™ DC Comics and Warner Bros. Entertainment Inc. (s17).
Published in 2017 by Mad Libs, an imprint of Penguin Random House LLC.

MAD LIBS® is fun to play with friends, but you can also play it by yourself! To begin with, DO NOT look at the story on the page below. Fill in the blanks on this page with the words called for. Then, using the words you have selected, fill in the blank spaces in the story.

Now you've created your own hilarious MAD LIBS® game!

PYRAMID SCHEME

NOUN _____

VERB _____

ADJECTIVE _____

PLURAL NOUN _____

PERSON IN ROOM _____

SILLY WORD _____

PLURAL NOUN _____

ADJECTIVE _____

PLURAL NOUN _____

VERB _____

NOUN _____

VERB ENDING IN "ING" _____

ADJECTIVE _____

ANIMAL (PLURAL) _____

VERB _____

PLURAL NOUN _____

OCCUPATION _____

MAD LIBS

PYRAMID SCHEME

Beast Boy needs cash to buy a/an _____ for Cyborg, so he
                                        NOUN

decides to _____ a pyramid scheme. This is when you sell
                 VERB

a/an _____ product, and the people who sell it for you give
         ADJECTIVE

you money. But to get started, you have to give lots of _____
                                                              PLURAL NOUN

to the people above you. Cyborg, Starfire, and _____ get
                                                    PERSON IN ROOM

cowboy badges to join. Robin says, "_____," since money
                                          SILLY WORD

only comes from honest _____. Soon, they are all so
                            PLURAL NOUN

_____, they don't know what to do with their mountains of
    ADJECTIVE

_____! So, they _____ money salads! Trouble
  PLURAL NOUN   VERB

arises when the boss of the _____ scheme comes
                                   NOUN

_____ for more money! A/An _____ pyramid
VERB ENDING IN "ING"   ADJECTIVE

rises from the ground. Mummies and _____ march out,
                                         ANIMAL (PLURAL)

and the Titans are forced to _____ on the pyramid! It takes all
                                  VERB

the _____ the Titans have to break free. Lesson learned:
        PLURAL NOUN

Mummies are scary, but being a/an _____ is fun!
                                        OCCUPATION

MAD LIBS® is fun to play with friends, but you can also play it by yourself! To begin with, DO NOT look at the story on the page below. Fill in the blanks on this page with the words called for. Then, using the words you have selected, fill in the blank spaces in the story.

Now you've created your own hilarious MAD LIBS® game!

SILKIE

ADJECTIVE _____

PLURAL NOUN _____

VERB _____

COLOR _____

ADJECTIVE _____

A PLACE _____

PART OF THE BODY _____

VERB _____

ADVERB _____

PART OF THE BODY _____

TYPE OF FOOD _____

PLURAL NOUN _____

ADVERB _____

ADJECTIVE _____

VERB ENDING IN "ING" _____

NOUN _____

VERB _____

SILKIE

Silkie (also known as Larva M3-19) is Starfire's _____ pet. He
ADJECTIVE

was originally part of Killer Moth's army of mutant _____,
PLURAL NOUN

which were created to overthrow and _____ Jump City. The
VERB

plan failed, and Beast Boy took Silkie to Titans Tower. Silkie looks like

a/an _____ worm with _____ eyes. He is allergic to
COLOR   ADJECTIVE

berries from (the) _____, which make his
A PLACE

_____ _____ if eaten! He _____ likes to
PART OF THE BODY   VERB   ADVERB

be licked behind the _____, too. Silkie eats canned
PART OF THE BODY

_____ and then barfs _____. It's a wonder he's
TYPE OF FOOD   PLURAL NOUN

still alive, but he is _____ the luckiest member of the
ADVERB

_____ Titans. He avoids trouble all the time without even
ADJECTIVE

_____! Plus, his _____ for Starfire has no
VERB ENDING IN "ING"   NOUN

equal. He'd _____ just about anything for her!
VERB

MAD LIBS® is fun to play with friends, but you can also play it by yourself! To begin with, DO NOT look at the story on the page below. Fill in the blanks on this page with the words called for. Then, using the words you have selected, fill in the blank spaces in the story.

Now you've created your own hilarious MAD LIBS® game!

ROBIN'S PERSONAL AD

ADJECTIVE _____

ADJECTIVE _____

VERB _____

PLURAL NOUN _____

NOUN _____

ADJECTIVE _____

VERB ENDING IN "ING" _____

ADJECTIVE _____

COLOR _____

NOUN _____

ADJECTIVE _____

PART OF THE BODY _____

A PLACE _____

VERB _____

NOUN _____

ADJECTIVE _____

PERSON IN ROOM (FEMALE) _____

ROBIN'S PERSONAL AD

Boy Wonder looking for _____ love.
                         ADJECTIVE

I am average height with a/an _____ build. I like to keep in
                               ADJECTIVE

shape, so I exercise and _____ a lot. Also, I'm an expert at
                          VERB

martial arts and _____. I drive a motorcycle and a/an
                  PLURAL NOUN

_____. I am a little obsessive and _____ about
   NOUN   ADJECTIVE

everything I do, but anything worth doing is worth _____
                                                   VERB ENDING IN "ING"

right! Right? I'm looking for a tall, _____ girl with pink hair,
                                       ADJECTIVE

orange skin, and _____ eyes. A purple _____ is
                  COLOR   NOUN

preferred, as are _____ ears. It would help if you could fly and
                   ADJECTIVE

shoot Starblasts from your _____. It wouldn't hurt if
                           PART OF THE BODY

you were the Princess of (the) _____, either! Now that I
                                A PLACE

_____ about it, there is only one _____ for _____
   VERB   NOUN   ADJECTIVE

Wonder, and her name is _____!
                        PERSON IN ROOM (FEMALE)

MAD LIBS® is fun to play with friends, but you can also play it by yourself! To begin with, DO NOT look at the story on the page below. Fill in the blanks on this page with the words called for. Then, using the words you have selected, fill in the blank spaces in the story.

Now you've created your own hilarious MAD LIBS® game!

THE ADVENTURES OF LADY LEGASUS

ARTICLE OF CLOTHING _____

ADJECTIVE _____

VERB _____

PART OF THE BODY _____

PLURAL NOUN _____

VERB _____

CELEBRITY _____

ARTICLE OF CLOTHING _____

ADJECTIVE _____

PART OF THE BODY (PLURAL) _____

PART OF THE BODY _____

VERB _____

VERB ENDING IN "ING" _____

THE ADVENTURES
OF LADY LEGASUS

When Robin steals Raven's _____, Raven discovers her

ARTICLE OF CLOTHING

legs have _____ abilities. She can kick and _____ with

ADJECTIVE — VERB

super power and sometimes even a third _____ shows

PART OF THE BODY

up to defeat her _____! She can even _____ with

PLURAL NOUN — VERB

her toes! Raven decides to leave the Titans and become Lady Legasus.

She easily defeats Cinderblock, Brother Blood, and _____,

CELEBRITY

but returns to the Titans when she discovers Cyborg has turned dark

from wearing her _____. Another time, Lady

ARTICLE OF CLOTHING

Legasus helps the Titans strengthen their _____ legs, and they

ADJECTIVE

form the League of _____! Lady Legasus is the

PART OF THE BODY (PLURAL)

leader, but there's also Thunder Thighs, Incredible Quad, Captain

_____, and The Calf. So, don't just work out that

PART OF THE BODY

upper body. Be sure to _____ with your legs, too! They're

VERB

important, and not just for _____!

VERB ENDING IN "ING"

Download Mad Libs today!

Join the millions of Mad Libs fans creating wacky and wonderful stories on our apps!